WHOA!

Are They Glad You're in Their Lives?

PRAISE FOR

WHOA! Are They Glad You're in Their Lives?

"We all need an Allan Cox in our life, someone who energizes us to higher planes. *Whoa!* will make you think and reflect and smile and grow. In this delightful book, Allan will spark your senses through a unique combination of photography, poetry, and gems of wisdom. It will inspire you to pause, take a deep breath, be peacefully present, and reconnect with your genuine self before charging on with renewed purpose."

> Amanda Montgomery
> Investment Officer, Head of Public Markets
> San Diego City Employees' Retirement Systems

"Allan Cox, I know, has been thinking all his life, as a student, college teacher, successful businessman, advisor, and consultant to anyone who needed his wisdom, about big questions of meaning, purpose, life and death, vocation, and authenticity. He has produced a truly remarkable resource that is much more than a "how-to" book. His daily thought-starters come from his own wide experience and from his own heart. His poems are simply and eloquently phrased and grounded in the daily mysteries and joys of the life we all live. The photographs alone are worth a leisurely and extended visit.

Along the way, Allan invites his readers to slow down, to remember, to cherish precious relationships and experiences, to live our one and only lives with alertness, awareness, and intentionality."

> John M. Buchanan
> Editor & Publisher
> *The Christian Century*

"Treat yourself to the pearls of wisdom scattered throughout Allan Cox's new book *WHOA! Are They Glad You're in Their Lives?* This insightful collection of tweets, poetry, and photography empowers us to come of age and notice what we are creating in our day-to-day lives. Written in manageable bits and pieces to savor each day, it's chock-full of insight and delight. Enjoy!"

> Eileen Chambers, PCC
> Personal Development Coach
> Eileen Chambers Coaching

"A curious and delightful mix of social media, photography, and poetry. Strange bedfellows, indeed, and sure to inspire you in multiple ways."

> Diane Lockward,
> Author of *Temptation by Water*

"I have had the opportunity to work with Allan Cox for the last few years on my executive development.

This professional relationship gave me the chance to work through his full range of professional development activities, most of which are contained in the executive development books he's written over the years. This experience not only taught me to be a better performing, more mature executive, but provided deep insights into what is most significant in my life, both professional and personal.

As our business relationship grew into a friendship, I became exposed to another side of Allan that exceeds and supplements his remarkable business acumen. Showing this side, he delves fearlessly into the meaning of one's life, one's purpose, the intertwining of one's relationships and gives guidance for peering into what the next phase of life might bestow.

WHOA! is a little book that probes that other, more complex side. It provides the reader with a unique opportunity to ponder the cumulative insights on life and the wisdom of a truly remarkable sage in our midst.

For those (most of us) who sometimes find themselves flooded by the amount of data to master in today's work world, *WHOA!* doesn't disappoint. It's efficient and concise. It allows readers to develop a daily or weekly habit to get themselves on the path of meaningful personal reflection."

Dominic Dannessa
Senior VP and Chief Technology Officer
USG Corporation

WHOA!

Are They Glad You're in Their Lives?

Allan Cox

Harrier Press

Harrier Press

Harrier Press

Harrier Press
980 North Michigan Avenue
Chicago, IL 60611

Book design, front cover, back cover design, editorial, typeset by Big B Consulting

First edition published 2012

Manufactured in the United States of America

10 9 8 7 6 5 4 3 2 1

Library of Congress Cataloging-in-Publication Data

Cox, Allan
        WHOA! Are They Glad You're in Their Lives?,
                p. cm.
        1. Leadership. 2. Executive ablity. 3. Coaching. 4. Self-Growth. 5. Poetry.

ISBN 978-1-938610-02-8

DEDICATION

For Marvin and Nancy Hiles, Iona Center

"That which is unique and worthwhile in us makes itself felt only in flashes. If we do not know how to catch and savor the flashes, we are without growth and without exhilaration."

—Eric Hoffer

Horse

I don't know what
it was about you
that caught me,
more than my eye.
It was a body-long shaft,
an abrupt instant,
an explosion, force
almost beyond reckoning
that brought me still as death.
All seen in that moment
frozen in your stance,
head whipped firm
by knowing eyes, shining,
utter captive to the scent.
Now, rear up on
those hard round haunches,
turn on steel legs
and tear, extending,
with all bonds broken,
as only you can,
for home.

For Nag Arnoldi

Contents

WHOA! Are They Glad You're in Their Lives?

Sona Chawla
President, E-commerce
Walgreen Co.
Deerfield, IL

FOREWORD

How often do you stop to take a 360-degree view of your life and heed a call-to-action to live in an authentic way? To be authentic, you don't need to be perfect, but you can aspire to have a substantial impact on your circle of colleagues, family, friends, acquaintances, and even strangers. *WHOA! Are They Glad You're in Their Lives?* is a book that guides you to come of age—as an executive, a parent, a spouse, and anything else you are or genuinely want to be.

Brief, provocative, and tweetable, this is a book appropriate for our times from a message and medium perspective. Our daily lives are so complicated today as we balance competing demands, sip from a fire hose of information, and navigate an increasingly turbulent economic landscape. With the growth and proliferation of technology, more and more information flows into our lives. Every minute, 42 million new pages are added to the World Wide Web, 168 million emails are sent, and more than 25 hours of video content is generated on You-Tube. Unprecedented access to this burgeoning information has a bipolar impact, expanding our horizons while simultaneously insulating us by bringing information into our hub. A book that helps us radiate externally and focus on our connections to others is timely indeed.

To help you start, Allan Cox gives you a frame connected by 365 thought-provoking statements, but the house you build on it is custom and uniquely yours. There is no spoon-feeding, as this is not a book for the languid mind. You have to work and dig deep, so if you see your life as a continuous evolution, pour a little of yourself into this book each week and see what you get. Each chapter culls insights and nuggets of wisdom from Allan's rich and diverse career as a successful CEO advisor, author, poet, and executive recruiter. And like a meeting with Allan himself, each chapter sparks your thinking and gives a gentle nudge to guide you along.

In a meeting I had with Allan a few months ago, he said, "Two things mark a superior executive—judgment and timing." His timing was perfect and perhaps unbeknownst to him, he had given me a gift. I had just come from a session where I had presented a new idea to my colleagues and had been met with resistance. Frustrated, I had wondered "Why don't they see it the way I do; isn't it obvious?" No, it was not. I had not seasoned the idea yet. I had to wait, stop selling, and lose the emotion. I retracted, reworked, and waited for the right time, then presented the facts with less emotion and more empathy. The results were so much better. As Allan says, "People with no agenda can go where there is no space. Somehow there is room for them."

If you want to gain entry into the crowded lives of those whom you care about and leave a lasting, positive impact, then I highly recommend that you read this book. Set an authentic goal and start your journey.

Sona Chawla
President, E-commerce
Walgreen Co.
Deerfield, IL

Introduction:
What This Book Can Mean to You

This is a book I've wanted to write all my adult life, but wasn't old enough, didn't know enough. Its aim is to teach readers how to understand *and* express themselves so that they can get inside the lives of the people they care about most. Belong. Add value. For you, that includes the family you came from *and* the one you want to build; the people you rub shoulders with at work—the bosses, the colleagues, the subordinates, customers and suppliers—the old friend who's slipped off your radar, the beloved aging neighbor. All these contribute to a life that only you can navigate and take pride in. The life you want to have *must* be genuine, uniquely yours, truly understanding of yourself and how/why you interact in relationships. Your deepest desire is to be loved and loving it, making your contribution seamlessly, knowing how to do this in an everyday way.

The book's structure is an unusual collection of tweets, pictures, and poems: 7 tweets per week—for 52 weeks on challenges everybody faces; then a compelling photograph that invites you to ponder; then an accessible poem from me to provide a new angle. Some of its topics and ideas, like life itself, overlap and intertwine. You may find the seven daily tweet-like takes each week come at you either too routinely or seem too crowded. If that's so, move on or slow down as it suits you and make the "year" as long or short as you need. Do what's best for you.

The "artsy" aspects of the book may make you wonder if it could be fun just to breeze through—you know—like beach reading. It's *definitely* not that. It really is an invitation to those bent on lifelong learning to see the seven weekly takes as thought-starters, a furthering of a life of inquiry. Good stuff . . . contemplating how you want your life to be and mastering the tools to get you to that place. Go! Range far and wide. Learn lessons where you don't expect to find them.

All quieted minds are waiting minds; not all waiting minds are quiet. Think about that. If your mind isn't quiet, genuine thoughts just won't come. Slow down . . . wait. Start the process each week; when you get into a groove, fresh new ideas and sparks will fly.

I love the old adage "If you don't know where you're going, any road will take you there." As far as I know, we've only got one shot at getting it right in this life. Start down your own unique path, using this book as a road map. See where your imagination, your head, and your heart take you.

Structure

The weekly fast-takes are for intelligent, committed people who insist on creating their own structure and care about continual enlightenment and personal growth. There are 365 tweets—all of which matter in a life. Personalize them. See them as eye-openers, reminders of what you already know that may need a new context.

The material, initially, may seem soft, but the truths you learn about yourself are *hard.* Consider this: If you get one insight from this activity—something of real merit that you can apply to your life—wouldn't it be worth it? Ideas lead to self-discovery and, often, change. Seek out some uncomfortable scenarios, "try on the dress," see how it feels. Soul searching and reflection lead to the joy of discovery. Early in my career, I was a teacher. Teachers like to coax out what's already inside, waiting to be discovered. You need a quieted mind and a little time to start *your* discovery.

If I were to come at this book as a stranger, I'd bear down as I normally do, grab a yellow pad and start reading—seeing where it takes me. For your convenience, we've included a sample Worksheet at the back of the book as a guideline.

Keep your notes, throw them into your computer, or keep the yellow pad intact—to revisit as you grow and learn more about who you really are. Free up your mind. Let images pop into your head. How does the photo relate to the poem? What does any of it have to do with the tweets and how you see yourself in the world? There are no wrong answers, just wonderful interpretations. You might even want to create a Weekly Study Group at the office and share ideas.

Why poetry? All those funny, little lines. I started writing poetry in 2009, though I've been reading it daily for about five years. I think of it as the CliffsNotes of human understanding. I know of no medium anywhere near its equal for providing more with less. Its economy dumbfounds me. Short stories, brilliantly told by writers of every shape, sphere, and temperment. Its subtlety honors my mind while it feeds my soul. It also teaches me to use words better.

Poetry doesn't have to be as inaccessible as many writers have made it. Try it here. See if it takes you beyond the clichés. Intrigued? Let me recommend a side study that will wake you up alongside this book. Get hold of *Good Poems*, edited by Garrison Keillor, available in paperback. It's a fabulous collection of accessible moving works, with an introduction by him that will crack you up. He shows, as only he can, that much so-called good poetry isn't good and that poetry that's good can be written by people most of us haven't heard of. I love poetry, didn't know that I did, and wonder if perhaps that may be true of you.

Summing up in as few words as possible, this book is a skeleton. Its flesh comes from you. It will build your poise. Poise really matters.

Allan Cox

Being human cannot be borne alone.

—*John Updike*

ther-centeredness is much more than a do-good
notion. It ensures our enriched survival. Take away our
linkages to what enfolds us—other beings, the material
and nonmaterial, nature in all its forms along with our
gratefulness for their richness and contribution. Take
away our standing by those linkages. Then see that we
suffer unbearable isolation, life that lacks the capability to
meet the challenges of a complex world. Family, friends,
factories, fields and streams, coworkers and neighbors,
strangers toward whom we're moving, or will—this is the
human inborn disposition: ties that bind. Too many fail
to step up onto this building block and instead fall into a
boiling stew-pot of self-reference. This oversight taints lives
across the social fabric and threatens danger to the loner's
health—physically and emotionally. Reach out. Let in. This
is the true nurturing of self.

Week 1

What It Means to Be Self-Assured

1. You don't make things happen as much as you let them happen.

2. Moderation and poise come with time, but you can start early.

3. You don't just ask questions, as critical as that is; you also make statements bargained between your head and your heart.

4. Initiative may mean waiting. Don't make decisions before their time.

5. You have a clearly articulated life purpose, one that quickens your spirit.

6. People sense, but may not know that you are (1) other-centered, (2) courageous, (3) judicious, and (4) resourceful.

7. You enjoy periods of silence.

Riddle

Do you know
what makes her special,
that she hires people
better than she is?

Because,
most often,
they don't.

Something inside her—
fearlessness that throws its arms around
superiority—that can make tasks
and people and air and beliefs and herself—
stir.

She does it again and again
as her work grows green and leafy.
She has her disciples,
surprisingly few.

Week 2

Find Your Model

8. Models are so good they don't know it.

9. Models teach us not by what they say but by the way they behave, the way they move.

10. Models often don't know they're models, won't even accept the title.

11. Models are masters.

12. Models know how to be quiet.

13. Models invest themselves wholly in the process, the organization, the goal, and their people.

14. Models leave legacies.

Janitor

A bit rotund and bald,
he smoked a pipe,
took care of his job,
calm in what he was about.
Routine problems
in our classrooms
he dispatched
in our absence
so as not to distract.
But at Christmas
was everywhere
setting up trees to
a child's delight—
their standing firm, green,
ready for our trimming.
He spoke, was friendly
but kept his distance
in his pace.
I ventured, though,
and found him before

the opening bell,
for a few minutes
to share in his pad,
so warm and toasty,
among the basement
rigging, puffing pleasant.
He sat high in a chair
with full view
of the playground
out three wide windows
and saw all the kids
in their moves.
He surprised me—
knew them all by name,
knew who cheated
and those who shared,
those cold, those who cared,
knew the athletes,
knew the siblings,
knew a lot,
my new friend.

Week 3

See the Wonder of Small Things

15. Subtle events, small things, often have the most meaning. They blend in, one after another, without rigging for our attention.

16. Years ago on January 1, I'd declare, "This is the big one for me." It seemed so, yet now it doesn't satisfy and I mind my little years.

17. Note your little affections. They'll give hints to your life theme. You may not like the trajectory, but you'll know what it is.

18. So-called little decisions in your organization give hints of its trajectory. String them together. Ask: "Is this for me?" "Good for us?"

19. Big decisions are more easily reversed. They can be seen more plainly, are on a grand scale. See the little ones, the quiet momentum.

20. Make a big contribution to your team by getting them to think small. The meaning of small things yields deep insights.

21. *Valor* and *value* come from the same root, *val,* meaning "worth." Multiply your worth by showing valor in the little things.

Filament

You, there, filament inside the softening globe.
I pull the shade off your little lamp—
those useful-but-ugly small clamps that enfold you
catch my eye, and I let it pass.

I put the shade down and press you on with my thumb,
cup both my hands around you,
wait to see how long it takes for you
to be too hot to handle.

You are one of the *trillions* of light bulbs—
a light nonetheless—let us never forget!

Oh, Filament, Oh, Filament
How lovely are your sunbeams . . .

Who thought you up? Edison?
He certainly gets the credit.
How he loved you.
How inhumanly tirelessly
he spent himself to bring you forth,
sampling fiber after fiber,
finding, finally, what gives you life
and makes you shine.

Early, you were spare and dim and one.
Today, you're legion and encased
in that cloudy globe and its climate.
I see that's a two-way protection:
Your glare diminished in the space you give,
spared harm from lack of care.

He was the one, wasn't he? Edison?

Week 4

Appreciate Your Parents

22. My parents brought three older siblings and me into the world and provided for us. We bear their mark.

23. I appreciate my parents' stoicism. They were deep country farm types. From them I learned how to accept bad news with poise.

24. They taught me to laugh. My dad told funny stories, was good on dialects. My mother was an encourager yet cut me down to size.

25. They gave me a faith I haven't retained but a grounding claimed, like Jacob wrestling with the angel, filled with promise.

26. My dad found work all through the Depression. We never missed a meal. He showed me how to make do.

27. I've forgiven myself for oblivion at my parents' unconditional love and grateful for what I can't know: all the things they did for me.

28. Forgive your parents. There's no such thing as a nondysfunctional family. They did the best they could.

Parents

It seems possible
to overrate
the impact of
our parents
on whom we've become.
Models of virtue
give rise
to slugs and sinners.
Out of the homes
of reprobates and absentees
come swans and singers
who find and create
a wealth of environs
that nourish them.
Prediction readily defied,
what matters most,

perhaps,

is to claim in heart
what your parents
gave that you wove
wittingly, unwittingly
as you composed
your world's walk
masterpiece.

Week 5

Pay Tribute to Unsung Heroes

29. People cite who *most* moved their lives with titles of parent, grandparent, other relative, school teacher, coach, priest, and the like.

30. My dog, Princess, was run over by a train, and I thought I would die, too. By nightfall, though, with my Dad's help, I was laughing with friends.

31. Mrs. Cudney, a neighbor, taught me—a callow youth—that when you tell a lie, you usually have to tell three or four more to cover it.

32. Be awake to people who touch you deeply. What is it about them that's about you?

33. What is worth learning and mastering? Forget everything else—that's where you must go. Who, really, tipped you off to that?

34. Sometimes the most valuable thing done for me is that I've been ignored.

35. Next time you're in front of a fireplace, sit down, look quietly into the flames. Who comes to mind?

She

Some people ask,
What would Jesus do?
and I'm OK with that;
after all he was who he was.
Bringing that idea
down to the tactile,
it's that person—
to you and me,
to our friends, family
and co-workers—
who inserts herself
into our lives
by her absence.
What leads to the lingering?
She laughs, she frowns,
she asks the right questions,
she declares herself
in the right way.
She goes before us.
She comes after us.
She goes away
and never leaves.

Week 6

How Do People See You?

36. *What's in it for me?* We all ask that. What's hard to take in us, though, is when that's what we ask most.

37. Do you participate? Are you there, really *there?* Engaged? Are you idling when you should be in gear?

38. Woody Allen says you can outperform 80 percent of the people by just showing up.

39. I saw a coffee mug once that read, "Pardon me, but you've mistaken me for someone who gives a shit."

40. If habitually you stop in your tracks, afraid of making a mistake, how can you ever be *you?* How can you ever be seen as *real?*

41. We don't expect our bosses to be error-free, always on good behavior. We're most happy when we feel they're real.

42. The word of choice in recent years for describing executives we respect is *gravitas.* It's a good one: "dignity of manner."

Side

The side angle face,
what does it show?
Photographers work
with it all the time
and no doubt have
rich answers.
But what does it
reveal to you and me
with our untrained sight?
My preference is to see
stillness,
not just as in a
photograph—
as that can be
nothing but a face
caught in an instant.
I like stillness
over many instants,
not necessarily fierceness—
though that's alright—
but a face in the presence
of substance
and takes it in
with a quiet eye.

Week 7

Settle into Your Plainness

43. Doing the obvious is so difficult. Why? The question is profound in its simplicity. If it were easy, we'd all be doing it.

44. Doing the obvious—fundamentals—is to care enough to find true purpose in the mundane. If you can't do this, you're not plain enough.

45. How about your voice? Do you have control of it? Strained? Raspy? Too high, low, breathy, thin? Does it put one at ease? Voice tells.

46. Shortcuts? Tricks of the trade? Inside dope? All the wrong questions! The plain one: Into what, precisely, will you pour yourself?

47. Has your boss taught you a lot? Take a moment for that to settle. Next week, find a way to tell her. Simple, easy, grateful, real.

48. Everyday heroes measure themselves against the most basic behavioral benchmarks. Add them up and you'll have something special.

49. Satisfy yourself that you're comfortable in your own skin.

Art

The folds and curves
in a great stone sculpture
or carving in wood
are a marvel attuned
to a life lived well.
The particulars in
the quality of life
of the sculptor,
may escape us,
but in his work,
masterfully done,
we can glimpse
the complexity borne,
the patience practiced,
the discipline to what is
as the life of a thing—
like the purpose of a life—
emerges, never fully seen,
till looking backward.
The startle of belief,
the bared soul,
the spirit of lostness,
the joy in the labor,
the finding of the way.

Week 8

What Have You Overlooked?

50. It's so easy to look away from what works for me every day. Tying my shoes, for instance.

51. A new survey shows half of Americans don't attend religious services. That means every other person I meet does.

52. See the opportunity for making a statement instead of asking a question to which you already know the answer. Declare!

53. "If everyone would sweep in front of his own door, the whole world would be clean." —*Goethe*

54. I think I'll just sit here for a time on this park bench.

55. Have you seen the boots beside the beds in the firehouse?

56. Did you know high-tech serves low-tech? The cockpit of an airliner is a tiny part of its structure

Hydrant

You may not have noticed,
not all fire hydrants
are stocky—short and stout.
They're not all red either.
Many are tall and thin, dressed

in colors like rust and yellow and black.
You may hardly have noticed hydrants at all—
a tool of human development—

brilliant as planet Venus in their simplicity,
stoic as sentries in their caring.

The concept started in ancient China
when big pots of water were placed
around villages.

The American version,
closer to what we see today,
began in Philadelphia in 1802.

Hydrants go Hollywood with supporting roles
in movies in fire and rescue scenes, and in comedies
and dramas where inner city kids find

intriguing uses for them. Cute, but most apt for your
thoughts is the hydrant's nickname:

Fireplug,

unglamorous heroism,
constant presence,
silent service,
power outlet

for instant use,
receding gracefully into the background
after giving, giving, giving.

Week 9

Look to the Hills

57. Straight from her, the CEO's assistant: *The 4-F game is (1) focus, (2) figure it out, (3) finalize, and (4) forward HO.* Lucky, her boss!

58. Waiters lacking peripheral vision fail. Same story with executives. Same story with parents.

59. Face up to the real issue. Rearranging all the beer glasses won't produce champagne.

60. The hard work of a lifetime can't equal the true talent of an hour. But true talent is often a truant.

61. Don't visit a great museum with your sights set on its tearoom.

62. Four stages of any organization: 1. birth and creativity 2. power and growth 3. obsolescence and decline 4. rebirth or death.

63. Are you on course for distinctive performance? No? Then who will believe in you? Nothing moves without this.

Habitat

What works? What's mine?
What's undeniable but
unseen to my untrained eye?
Look, look! Take the training.
John Burroughs wrote,
"To find new things,
take the path you took
yesterday."
Constraint, my mentor,
where I belong,
free and forceful
as the crow's caw—
if I look.
Not till today
did I look
and look back
to see where
within the wires
I withhold my
yes.

Week 10

Hey, You, Kid,
From the Wrong Side of Town!

64. Poor kids learn more than rich kids. If they succeed, they've come further.

65. Struggling through college, and a rich kid invites you for the weekend? Go! You'll return with new deposits in your training bank.

66. Take stock of your emotional strengths; they are many. You know—what you've got inside that's yours alone.

67. Stay close to that mentor-sponsor who has so much to do with where you are today. Never stop being grateful. Pass it on.

68. When your professor asks for volunteers, be the first to raise your hand.

69. Smell opportunity. Bite off more than you can chew, and chew it. *This* is a time for sense of urgency.

70. Study those who work well with people. Do what they do.

Tufts

They're the clumps of grass that grow up between the cracks
in the sidewalks of spurned-dead neighborhoods in any big city
in America. Go, pal, walk their streets at

mid-day, past the gas stations, the mom and pops, liquor stores,
bars, strip malls, greasy spoons, dry cleaners and store fronts—
oh, all of those—some still breathing, more of them shot with
sucked-up resources or hoped-for promise that wore thin. Cut
across the empty lot with its ground-down path that splits its four

square corners into two rude triangles with surfaces that look
like a Jackson Pollock painting with a hangover: A thin-spread
inlaid cracked glass patina, sleazy adornment of empty beer
bottles, varied wino discards, weather-beaten boxes, flung
away alley condoms, rags and bags of all sorts, a car part

or two, one empty shoe and even a quick-ditched sawed-off
shotgun. Take the time, man, to roll by where people live—
the old apartment buildings that need tuck-pointing, and the
bungalows—drill-instructed soldiers called to attention—clucked
tight, a block-after-block regiment, then on past them to see
hookey-drones and dropouts on some of the corners, and see the

cruising squad—its cops putting the look on you, doubting
your business here. Then, for sure, take in the schools, a
couple of them. Bend your ear sharp beside their mixed-race
playgrounds: hear some laughing—open n' lopin' past the blight,

the always-there bully, wrong-way pointers, and the sly pusher.
There are *teachers* behind those walls—not all are slobs or cynics!
And churches or synagogues, same story there: Rabbi, Sunday school
    teacher,
some nun with an open-door heart, and a preacher who shoots
hoops at the playground or park. The streets mostly are quiet and

men and women—parents, married, single, divorced—despite
nasty job prospects, do their work wherever they can find it to
help them and their kids make it. The tufts here say what this
neighborhood is like: a statistical pattern you can figure from the
first pudgy clump. The numbers say that it's kids who grow up,
leave—almost never coming back—who make something of themselves,
give credit to their moms. But out of this weed-filled garden—and get
it right, this is a garden—kids do flourish here and other places just like
everywhere. It's the *binding* that may give them spine that sets them free.
OK, let's say mom is prime dog, then comes that piloting angel—
    in the form

of another grown-up, maybe the teacher—who knows the waters, that
"My God, who-would-have-believed-it?" giver who feels she was made
for this time . . . and then, oh yeah, the kid, alone, with unspent ripe
    resources,
looking in the mirror in a dim bathroom, who wonders—with all the
    bullshit
and threats he's heard to the contrary—can I do this?

Week 11

Go to the Country

71. If you live in suburbia or the city, make good use of your parks. Also, whenever you can, air out your life by going to the country.

72. Nature is our teacher. It needs nothing from us to thrive, though it seems clear to me, as flower to bee, we are kin.

73. Just to be somewhere and hear crickets on a summer night from a porch or through an open bedroom window is a contrast that heals.

74. Stare at a rippling river, on your buns, leaning lazily under a tree for an hour or two. Notice the change in your disposition.

75. Snow-covered spruces standing tall together, emanating stateliness and ruggedness. How good it feels to be surrounded by them.

76. Bluffs on one side, the sea on the other, hard sand beneath my feet, I can walk for miles with just the sky as my ceiling.

77. The sound of the first birds of morning. Birdsong is Godsong.

Woods

As if I didn't know
I declare again,
there is a need for woods.
I feel it in ways
beyond the obvious—
when I'm there,
surrounded by fallen
leaves at the base
of dense trees,
that when I squint.
I convert them into
a thick layer of ash
and smell their burning.
It's a townie's version
built on memories of
rake scrapings, curbs
and happy dads communing
up and down the block
in the annual festival.
The oases are everywhere—
from the plane, cruising
30,000 feet up,
acres upon acres

of green, fallow or
snow-covered farmland
abutting or even surrounded
by compact neat woods,
all those trees standing like
marines, bending only
when I'm not looking.
A river runs through
a noisy city, but in places
one finds it tree-lined and
a wall alongside
you can lean over.
There in such a city
on my computer,
a screen calmly composed
of a dull red rowboat
moored on the bank of a small lake—
behind, a white frame cabin,
just into the clearing, helping
lift above its low roof
a white moon
into the gray sky.

Week 12

Go to the City

78. "Where do the children play?" —*Cat Stevens*

79. Let's say you grew up in the wrong part of town. Maybe you should go back for a visit. Maybe you could make the difference there for someone.

80. You name it! Pace, resources, talent, lights, restaurants, architecture, vastness—the complexity—a world of wonder and degradation.

81. In my city, there are three mega-university medical centers—such beehives—a lot of healing going on!

82. There's a lot of public poetry reading, too. Now, *there's* a timeless leavening influence that reaches beyond the city's borders.

83. Kids suffer in public schools, but teachers still exist there whose work win's God's smile.

84. The city's neighborhoods and their diversity are a special gift. Get into it.

Health

I hear the tenor whine
of a compactor on the
back of a garbage truck
in the alley.
It's a feat of design
engineering—that
compactor.
Does it have a soul?
Certainly soul went into
its design
and soul, no doubt,
if not regularly,
then surely occasionally,
goes into its operation.
The same you could say,
for those responsible
for its maintenance
and repair.
Its work is muscled
and clearing and smelly.

It makes room—
expands capacity,
increases production,
reduces labor,
number of trips,
and fuel consumption;
creates jobs,
lowers your civil taxes.
War is education.
Sanitation is health.

Week 13

Love That Special Person

85. It's nourishing to be loved, but special good fortune to share a life with someone who's won your heart. Love someone? That's your gift.

86. Difficulties and tensions between you and another are inevitable if you believe in yourselves, whole-self expression and lifelong learning.

87. *Together and separate* is the paradox to live, learn, experiment with, and relish—the growth in the other means growth in you.

88. Your barometer for knowing you've been wrong and inconsiderate is heartache. Feel the pain. Acknowledge your error. Fix it.

89. Harbor resentment? That's your way to keep score.

90. There's no substitute for affection—lots of it. You're made for love.

91. Thrive on your memories of glad times together. Stay fresh and keep them coming with what you do today.

Steps

1.

She frying eggs
in a big black skillet—
sizzling, smoke
going up
the exhaust fan.
The kitchen,
today a hard
summer rain
freshness
coming in
the open window
in the nook.
Grateful, their
love life
together.

2.

On the sidewalk,
waiting for her
to come out,
peering down
at a puddle
on the lawn,
left by
the burst
of rain.

3.

He goes to
the supermarket
with her.
While she's elsewhere
pushing her basket,
he lingers in produce
and his eyes
fall on the clumps
of asparagus,
each bound by
a red rubber band.
He's never noticed
this formidable assembly.
He picks up one,
surprised by its
heaviness.
He likes its
nubby surfaces.
He catches up
with her, smiles proudly
and places his bounty
in the basket.
She returns his smile
and says, "tonight."

Your boundaries are
your quest.
I could explain this,
but it will break
the glass cover
on your heart,
and there's no fixing that.

—*Rumi*

o reclaim what you care about and can master, you have
to get past your fears, your hesitating attitude. You can't be
good at what you do if you don't care, and you can't care if
you're not authentic. Think of something trivial to you — like
your boss asking you to plan and manage the company
picnic. You dread it, and like Moses, think someone else
could do it better. But you do it and find that it requires real
imagination to make it a success. You take to the task with
a coming appetite. Others love your attitude and your skill
at inspiring collaboration. People say it is the best ever,
something to look forward to next year. At the same time,
you discover new ambitions in yourself and see new ways
to put your leadership in play across your job. Not bad for a
task that scared you. Step forward.

Week 14

Stay Strong and Bounce Back

92. When you've failed, know that this is learning. No matter how bad it went, acknowledge the teaching. Soak it up.

93. How you handle failure is a key determinant of what your options can be afterward. Don't compound failure by being a jerk.

94. See poetry and color in your career: the hammers, feathers, leather, and lace. Embrace them all; find joy in the art of work.

95. Know the rhythm. When told you're good at something, smile, be animated, say "Thank you." "Oh, it was nothing" deprecates your worth.

96. You can't be good at what you do if you don't care, and you can't care if you're not authentic. Authenticity is maturity.

97. Be with true friends often to be strong when you're elsewhere not so accepting. They feed your self-worth, carry you past your doubts.

98. Meet your true test: resilience! First, last, and always—no matter how gifted you are—stick, finish, find a way.

Circle

Much of my life seems grokked from the middle.
What can I do to get off to the griddle?
Don't think that way, it's false and futile.
Look for excuses? Know they're all tootle!

When beginning this project
I knew was a risk,
when I started to fail,
what I heard was tsk-tsk.

Lo, in haste to the dungeon I fled,
lifted my palms and saw that they bled.
Despair would have me—
there wounded in terror—
yet I stiffened in truth and
and turned round to my error.

Here's what I said to the friend in the mirror,
The start takes courage, there's no doubting that,
but it's finding *true learning* comes calling with fate.
How do you with strength grasp the nettles to date?
Do you dismiss grit and go on your way?
Or commit your soul to learn how to stay?

Arrogance and hope are the comforts of loss.
Who better than you grasps the first thing to toss?
Say thanks to the skills that got you here,
but claim this, the wide middle—
as your ground to keep clear.

O, life is good, I figured it out.
I've grown where I needed and avoided a rout.
Yet might I grow headstrong,
and blow the whole thing?
No, No, say I and keep running the ring.

Week 15

Consider New Things

99. See lessons on work as they appear. Learn team effort by studying an ant colony. Be amazed by the rhythm of a skilled crane operator.

100. Wake up tomorrow by making your cells happy. Give thanks to your blood, water, and amniotic fluid. Where would you be without them?

101. For now, permanence is proof of adaptability. The moral: Keep scanning.

102. Achievers master the obvious. Do the obvious well, and others will ask, "Why didn't I think of that?"

103. For example, no outcome is more predictable than this: Firms with warmth attract and keep superior executives.

104. Vision is not clairvoyance; it's excavating the buried values of the organization—naming them, reclaiming them for its mission.

105. The executive known and loved for legacy is first and foremost a facilitator.

They

Sure, it sounds silly,
but I think of water as *they*.
How many drops in a cup of coffee?
How many tears in a good cry?
Did you know that in Japan,
school children wrapped labels
around jars of water with messages that faced inside—
one group saying I love you and the other I hate you?
Then they froze the water of each
under the direction of a scientist,
and the hate group made ugly ice crystals
and the love group made beautiful.

The scientist says water has memory,
and with all their experiences, I believe
they have stored deep learning
even before Big Bang.

My Swiss grand aunt's
great grandmother
drank a cup from a cistern.
Let's say they—the waters of it—
made the tortuous trip
to my mother's amniotic fluid,
and in turn to mine . . .

Imagine that the waters, subsiding gently,
leaving Noah's ark resting on Mt. Ararat,
now—with feeling—course through you.

Week 16

Become Your Own Person

106. We do different things for the same reasons and the same things for different reasons.

107. One musician works for pleasure, another for money; one composes for recognition, another performs for it.

108. Make no mistake, your competence is wrapped up in your resilience.

109. He asked me: "What do you have to offer that your competitors don't?" "Nothing," I replied. Saying so made me unique, and later I got to show it.

110. G. K. Chesterton said, "If a thing is worth doing, it is worth doing badly." Learning is a hard start.

111. Guilt expresses our good intentions. Good intentions substitute for performance. You are more and less than your good intentions.

112. Is who I think I am an act? Is what I think an act who I am? My money's on both.

Question

What is your question—
the one aimed at joy in your life?

You could say, I think, that
the hit song "What's it all about, Alfie?"
from the movie with Michael Caine some 40 years ago
is a start.

But that's about it.

I believe *your* question,
like mine,
is yours *alone,*
and you've wanted down deep
to ask it for a long, long time.

Where do you find *more*
to get beyond *start?*

Memories:
Your glee at three in front of the Christmas tree
Wetting your pants in shame in kindergarten
Breaking your arm falling off your bike
Deep love or coldness toward your parents
Winning the spelling bee
Making the varsity
Getting the part in the senior class play
Genius in photography club
Summa Cum Laude in college
Awe at your child's birth

Do the shadings and opposites
of such events and passages,
and then more,
point the way?
In some fashion, yes.

We grow, learn, succeed, fail,
take risks and absolve ourselves
of responsibility,
do heroic things.
get even,
forgive,
complain.

We change
and stay the same.

I wondered once,
no longer do,
if the question rests
inside our good intentions.
After all, mostly, they're
a stand-in for performance—
what Karen Horney brilliantly
dubbed "the tyranny of the shoulds."

No!
Both
your question
and answer
lie in some exhilaration you've *lived*—
no mater how fleetingly,
and let get away.

What is this longing—
this tip-of-the-iceberg *you*
that for years, decades, even,
your image has rafted past,
bundled up in its state-of-the-art parka
and triple-skin boots?

Take your time.
Answer.

Week 17

It's Time to Refigure

113. "Every answer is a new question," said Karl Rahner, late Catholic theologian who had major impact on the Second Vatican Council.

114. Know where you belong. A *New Yorker* cartoon shows two fish walking ashore. One says to the other, "This is where the action is!"

115. If you won't live the now, now, you won't live the future when it becomes now.

116. Your organization, seeking brutal truth, first faces two questions: (1) Who are we? (2) Where are we headed?

117. Be catalyst to finding answers to them by articulating the organization's *buried* values. Don't listen to your words—watch your feet!

118. Blow the bugle if you like what you see. Blow the whistle if you don't.

119. Then, look into each other's eyes; just say yes, yes, yes and go from there.

Messenger

Behold that old sink in a small enterprise, hardly
a centerpiece effort, but still taking up space in a
corner of the warehouse.

A wire soap dish hangs from the faucet, and a ragged
gray towel has its place dangling from a rusty rack at
the sink's side, and the faucet drips.

Do we talk about the faucet presenting itself as a
still-life scene, or the drip or just the sink—as its own story?
I say all—for a time.

You first, Sink, what gives you your life?
Why do you exist? Why haven't you been
yanked out or replaced?

Never mind. This is all of a piece, more a statement
of vitality lost, history with brown edges, business
sapped of juice from lost care.

Truly, it's that indomitable drip that most claims my attention.
It's a messenger, each, one-by-one then it's off to new life

Somewhere.

Week 18

Mysteries Are Everywhere You Look

120. Destiny isn't drafted, but revealed.

121. We are responsible for our actions, but not results. Results lie with Destiny.

122. Life is a mystery. You are here. Why? Contemplate the miracle of your own birth. You had little to with it.

123. Facing this barren, fallow time—feeling that nothing's happening? Go with it. Stay with it. Something good is afoot.

124. Seemingly arbitrarily, my parents gave me my name. *Allan* means "harmony." This pleases me. What does your name mean?

125. The person in the next room is waiting for you. What will come of it when you open the door?

126. Turn the day, and perhaps a life, into something special. Let some truth buried inside you make its appearance.

Destiny

The dark waters you entered
will part.
No powers of fear or treachery
will defeat you.
You came willingly,
conveyed into the swells
by summons of the divine source—
who spends all
your vitality.
You complied
without hesitation
because you *know*
you're *needed.*

You go not seeing past your entry,
grasping that through
adroit navigation,
failure's learning and
new-school imagination,
glimpses of the ultimate
will be revealed.
You go
scuttling envies,
worn-out hopes,
convictions and habits
and all getting.

You see stack on stack
events and circumstance
fold in on arrivals
at unexpected shores,
so you go on, full tilt,
assured
your reclaimed gifts,
and authentic will
are quickened to serve this
loved world's need
in the only way.

Week 19

Dark Night of the Soul

127. "The best way out is always through."
—*Robert Frost*

128. Wrapped tight with no footing, loneliness,
an implosion that to this day is unmatched.
Where do I turn?

129. He'd had a hard night. One shoe, high quality,
was in the gutter. I'll leave it there. He might
be back.

130. I have to start all over, knowing nothing. Let
me just lean backward against this rock.

131. When something gnaws at me and I don't
know or won't know what it is . . . Oh, there's
the rub isn't it? *Won't* know.

132. Like a spinning top, it flags though, and
wobbles, then spills itself completely, my little
symbol of command performance burnout.

133. Imagine those strong pregnant women on the
Overland Trail: *Nine miles and no grief makes a
great day.*

Night

Among other things,
night affords distance.
"I'd like to sleep on it,"
he says, to others
or just himself.
Clarity may come from the
simple elapse of time,
a stepping back for a clear image
of what's at stake;
the settling of an idea:
Yes. No. Wait.

But there's more . . .

amid the folds of sleep,
an array of experience can infuse
a coming disposition
running anywhere on a line—
crooked or straight—
from terror to peace.
Likewise, dreams and wakefulness
can generate the same range.
Run. Stay. Fly. Plunge.

Therapists to whom he's drawn
have a saying:

"To know the dream,
you have to know the dreamer."

He likes that knowing that he brings himself,
that he's not a visitation of forces.
He creates the dream,
and everything in it
is him.
Every foible or glow
of every character or object,
every movement or
its lack in any environment.
Any of it, all of it, start to finish.
Him.
Morning.
Revelation.

The Divine him (his higher self)
has jousted over purpose
with the him committed to his own harm.
A puzzling, symbolic contest language
Unwound that he can understand.

So, then, how does he treat wakefulness?

Revelry, when he nurses
eagerness or anticipation
of pleasure for the day ahead.

Joy, temporary, near an open window,
absorbing the sharp crack of lightning,
bending to the unearthly thunder that follows,
exulting in the downpour's coverage.
Safe, drifting back to sleep.

The haunt, when sleep won't come,
some brand
of his soul's dark night,
beckoning, insistent . . .
He eases out from the covers.
reaches for his robe,
goes to his favorite chair,
turns on the bright light,
gets fully awake,
waits,
looks,
listens for that voice.
His.

Week 20

When You Don't Have the Answers

134. We've acknowledged that mystery is all around us—a given.

135. The sea is powerful by being low. The rivers flow into it. Low is good because it knows how to receive gracefully, naturally. Low waits.

136. What happens when wait-and-see turns out to be cowardly?

137. What to do when the meticulous plan falls through?

138. Fork in the road, many unknowns either way. Should I just turn back?

139. Rainer Maria Rilke, the poet's poet, wrote that we may not be able to handle the answers, so live the questions.

140. In art, nature, and life, there are times when tangles are beautiful.

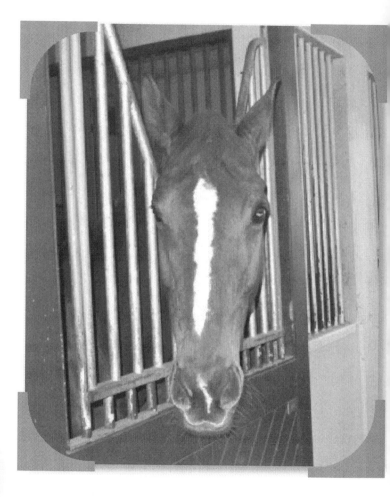

God

No less than
two decades ago
I encountered
a question
from a professor,
which gave me
a third eye.
He said, firmly,
"The question
is not
is there a God,
but what is God?"
For me,
that has made
all the difference.

Week 21

You and Your CEO

141. Nobody likes to fire people. That includes CEOs. They usually delegate this tough job to subordinates.

142. Are your CEO's sights set on the long-range health of the business rather than on her comp package and personal exit strategy?

143. Is your CEO rooted? Does she strike you as real, authentic? Does she make you proud? Take her measure.

144. See your long-term career options for what they are. Your CEO may or may not have it, and she's a key barometer for you.

145. To do well, companies have to do good. Does she want to do good?

146. If you see your job right, much is expected of you, for good reason.

147. Whether you stay or leave, now is the time to deliver.

Root

I am your root without a name
and am what makes you real—
like no other person.
Here in the dark, I can fool
and flood you with imagination.
Stay with me! You'll take within
your grasp three sustaining stones—
knowing they're your truth . . .

See that Chairman across the room,
talking with the tall woman?
He walked with me in the dark,
settled into his plain understanding:

I am here
Life welcomes me
My *purpose* is rounded movement

Today, he's a global treasure —
at home in his work,
joy to his people,
light to his customers,
friend to cultures.

Long lost, young years a shambles,
early work life blighted
by hurts and betrayals,
two marriages withered.

I waited—the drought nearly
killed us both.
He came to himself—
meaning he came to me,
and said, in time,
Life lived real is life
lived in surrender.

I'm not in your life as herald
of career, passions, image,
reputation, whatever,
whoever, wherever—
but living close
to the ground
today.

Week 22

Think Like a Child

148. I don't think people die; they just graduate.

149. I see people with grumpy faces, but I know there's something better in their hearts.

150. My widowed grandfather would bid me sit with him on the porch swing of his modest house. That was nice.

151. There's still nothing quite as good as a hot-fudge sundae.

152. Seven men mentored me by the time I was 24. That grounding set me for life.

153. The wind is whistling around our house, and has all night. That's a sound I love.

154. Blanche Oxborrow was our junior year American History teacher. Never was a teacher as good as she.

Miracles

**Spiracles
are miracles—
they're how**
grasshoppers
(and others)
breathe.
I don't know how
I breathe.
I just do
moment in,
moment out,
without thinking
about it.
I guess that's
taking it for granted
except for times
like this.
I guess, too,
if I were
to tap my mind
and take the time
I could write
a thousand pages
of miracles
just like this.

Week 23

Grown-Up Fantasies Work, Too!

155. Shakti Gawain wrote a classic book, *Creative Visualization*, that people love. You might like to read it, too. It can help open up possibilities.

156. Every once in a while, we have to ask ourselves, "What if water ran uphill?"

157. The wolf and sour grapes, Hansel and Gretel, Luke Skywalker and Obi-Wan Kenobi, Jack and the Beanstalk—my, what lessons they taught us!

158. My own favorite fantasy is *The Sound of Music*. What's yours? Look at little green Geico go!

159. How about the fantasy that comes true, like "My kid's off drugs!"

160. How about a prayer that just eased out of you?

161. What was the young Buddha-to-be *thinking* when he left home?

Adaptability

The train ran upside down
and backward
at full speed
on the bubble tracks.
It took off over the Rockies,
then plunged into the sea
to Neptune's Gardens.
When he saw me
he sank his pitchfork
into my heart
and I bled
blue cheese dressing.
A good thing that was, too,
because at dinner
it perked up
that wilting salad.

Week 24

Look for Signs and Symbols

162. Symbols are all around you, sending messages to your spirit that won't come from a book or even a close friend.

163. Nature is a rich source of symbolic messages. Countless! All you have to do is open your heart. Slow down.

164. The timing of events may seem arbitrary or capricious. Not necessarily. A door closes. Another opens.

165. Be about sensing; the seasons bring new rhythms, feelings, outlooks, light, and darkness to human flow.

166. What happens to you on a cold winter night, with a clear sky, when you look up to see a bright star almost poking you in the eye?

167. How about the animating phone call that you never expected? That rose garden in the park you don't see?

168. And that old friend who showed up from nowhere when you were flagging?

Density

There's a tree that enlarges nature and looks like ganglia—I mean
snaky synapse, making contact with an animating current—a leap

to life. At first glance, I saw in it a Quasimodo awkwardness that
quickly gave way to trust in its presence and goodness, to its core

and its name itself—The Valley Oak. It's not your every-day tree,
though no one can spurn the miracle of any tree. It's that this

one wraps my body into it; I would be left lonely only to look at it
without feeling myself solid in its impregnable density and see with

exuberance the shade it provides neighboring cows in blistering
summers.
My friend Marv took a stunning picture of this tree just past
dawn in the mist

of early spring in northern California, and simply seeing it
thrust me into
the folds of a visionary week, though its image in dark gray
light isn't sharp.

It fades as a ganglion ghost—gnarly, twisted branches and all—
    into the
hooded background of a muscled fence, twin posts side-by-side—
    a company

of them in a long line cradling rails between them; a protective
    bracing I've
never seen—a guardian brother holding dense faith alongside this tree's

massive trunk—all of it a piece, a bordered block of pulse churned
    full by an
abundance of groundwater and a root system to pierce the
    deepest mind.

This vibrant umbrella, buds budding, wider than tall,
    is on its way up past 100
feet, yet bending low, patient, ready to receive me, its density
    an availed purity.

I live like a king.
How can I be like this tree?

Week 25

A Different Kind of Courage

169. Go ahead, take a plunge into something you believe in. That's no guarantee your efforts will produce the results you expect.

170. You'd like to see around corners, but you can't. You trust your judgment. Sometimes that's not good enough, but doesn't mean you failed.

171. The results of your judgment aren't what you expected but *better?* Time to smile big and admit it. Your associates will love you for it.

172. You'll be amazed how much being at ease with yourself puts your associates at ease.

173. I once was asked sternly what I thought this one fellow had that his two main competitors for the top job didn't have. My answer: poise.

174. When things go bad—beyond your worst fears—your only course is to fess up; acknowledge the possibility of your hopped-up willfulness.

175. When you have success against the odds and recognize your intuition was your guide, recall humbly that's not entirely human.

Choice

I need to live by a different
kind of courage, one where
I go to the core of whatever
I'm part of,
but at peace with whatever
comes from it.

I'm not in charge.

Week 26

Danger Is a Fact of Life

176. We talk incessantly in business about risk, but where's the beef? Risk means fear. It's not an idle challenge. It can hurt.

177. We also speak critically of others as being risk-averse, but need to look in the mirror as we level this criticism.

178. Alfred Adler, a psychologist, said the three life tasks are work, love, and friendship. Doing well in each entails risk.

179. Encouragement does not mean mild, bland support but to *help make courageous.* This is one way we are our brother's keeper. Step in.

180. See, declare, and bite when your life is overrun with a hesitating attitude.

181. When you end up with egg on your face, people admire your acknowledging it and will help you work your way out.

182. "The ultimate leave-taking is leaving God for God." —*Meister Eckhart*

Danger

The *Tao Te Ching*
says there's a time
for being in danger.
Danger is personal—
that of the soldier,
> test pilot
> patient
> lover
> performer
> speaker
> investor
> friend
> decision-maker
> hang-glider
> parent
> jockey
> rock-climber
> child

I asked my wife,
"What is the most
dangerous thing
you've ever done?"
"Marry you,"
she replied.
So the *Tao* says danger
is a proper part
of life!
Makes me wonder
what ultimate trust
is.

One can do nothing now, forcing is disastrous.

—D. H. Lawrence

life that works is a life that moves point-to-point by judicious decisions. This doesn't mean that we labor over most decisions; typically, we make them successively in a relatively easy way based on grounded values. We've all faced circumstances in a complicated situation and been forced to choose between the lesser of two evils. Even in these times, we can ferret out the difference between the greater and the lesser. We call upon minds and hearts that discern the tradeoffs. Then we move ahead on a set of well-maintained visceral commitments. We hold up people who claim themselves this way as models of decision-making. That's because they reach clarity on issues and declare themselves accordingly. Get clear. Stay clear.

Week 27

Reflections Take Time

183. "Listening to stories makes you smarter."
—*Annette Simmons*

184. A better part of wisdom is to not walk into a room speaking.

185. I felt the loneliness of summer past and the gap that comes with fall not arrived.

186. "Poets don't make arguments; they reveal mysteries." —*M. Craig Barnes*

187. What does it mean that I remained silent in the meeting? Or that she did?

188. "I am exceptional," she declared, "and that itself is not."

189. Since becoming an adult (perhaps earlier), I have wanted to know my vital spark and call upon it to light my whole life.

Decree

Tangled branches,
two sets, bound,
fallen from the same tree
during last night's storm.
Soon the city truck
will come by
and pick them up
and grind them
on the spot.
Hear that sound!
The sentence of refuse.
That wouldn't happen
in the woods.
One could sit
on a fallen tree trunk
and pay attention to
them—notice their
entwining.

Week 28

Not All Is As It Seems

190. Come pre-fall, my friend tells me the crickets will begin singing in the daylight hours—even when the sun is high in the sky.

191. The paper on which she writes this very day marks the latest anniversary of civilization's birth.

192. How glorious to let the morning say itself.

193. Breakthroughs are ooze-throughs. All significant accomplishment is intergenerational.

194. Beware those missed times of saving grace when you refused to step back.

195. Present a yielding will. Then you will be meek and inherit the earth. You'll notice that inheritance is not yet granted.

196. My thumbnail is like a tiny mirror when I give the high sign. Do I really mean it?

Harvest

I, *Collaboration*, go to the field.
When I work with those who sweat,
there's no spoiling our efforts.
When people shed their false selves,
their fears of being known in a
way not known before
and become spendthrifts with their gifts—
gifts they doubted, but which, because
of me, they now claim boldly,

the clearing appears.
Imagine your task—outreach,
school, business, friends, governing,
health, recreation, communication—
and that you have brought together
a small core of people who want
to do right and bring their

talents to it.
I insist, if I am to be present,
and mark my words—
if I'm not, you'll likely fail—
that we have this understanding:
We not only don't expect to agree
on any issue that matters, but we won't

permit that.
Think about it—what's more absurd than
we gather bright, caring, well-trained,
done-their-homework contributors and
expect them to be of one mind on

issues of significance?
I'm not a concept. I'm to be grasped, in your face,
a little god, even, and just like the Big God
of the Old Testament, I'm jealous.
My devil and yours, too, should we choose
to go to the field together,
is, hear me, do hear me—

consensus.

O, come on, I know consensus is a given
in all discussions these days,
but I'm telling you, it's poison,
lacks courage and insufficient spadework.
Some decisions make themselves because we
can give them time, let them evolve.
Others are made by people who see things

because I'm there.
Lowest common denominator maneuvering
and group-think—real issues getting passed over,
and biting us in the ass later. That's what

consensus is.
So let me say it straight,
now that you're moving toward me:
Ripening won't come without true voice—
or as one sandpapery toiler puts it—
without fierce conversations.
Free-handed, we sow the seed of

the fertile field.
When I'm present, there's no dumb idea.
But are you ready for the paradox?
Our trust in each other, complete,
so that when your idea *is* dumb, and a toiler
has no hesitation saying so, you're not offended,
nor is she next day when she tries to flap

her broken wing.
Here's the secret: Pouring out your heart—
and anyone doing the same—may not win
the choice at the table's head this time,
but make no mistake, your pence pushes
clarity forward, *production* worthy

of the gods.
Do you want my mantra?
I give it freely, knowing its worth.

Collaboration without consensus
is the soul of organizational truth.

Week 29

It's What You Do When That Matters

197. Enthusiasm reflects confidence, spreads good cheer, raises morale, inspires associates, arouses loyalty, laughs at adversity—can't buy it.

198. Tech guru Alan Kay has said *perspective* is worth 80 IQ points. He couldn't be more right—a carload of smarts awaits you on the siding.

199. Relax—end of the workday—imagine a red field of wheat at sundown in the middle of nowhere, a glow that remains untold.

200. When I was 11, my sometimes hot-tempered dad said to me in the softest voice, "Son, you lied to me." Big impact. What's your lasting story?

201. Of all the qualities that mark the superior executive, two are most significant: (1) judgment and (2) timing.

202. People with no agenda can go where there's no space. Somehow there is room for them.

203. I've shaken my grateful head at how well things turned out when I had no choice. You don't always know when the *when* is taking place.

Bravery

Amy, young rookie in our contentious lab,
produced an experiment for sake of rehab.

We spurned what her small contraption would do—
two walls braced at their base as a wide flat U.

A tightly wound wire attached at both ends
was tested for strength and the message it sends.

Wire, clasp, walls, base, braces and wrench—
are space-age approved for George at the bench.

George grips the wrench and applies all his strength.
He grunts and tightens until at great length

beads pop on his forehead and his power fails.
Nothing collapses and a new world prevails.

As with wire, walls and base whole and secure
we'll reclaim lost resources on the ascending tour.

I looked long and deep into Amy's face,
then recalled a fragment from a poet's embrace.

It is William Carlos Williams who timely brings:
there is a small holiness/ to be found in braver things.

Week 30

Who Are You? You Thought You Knew!

204. Sense of urgency as a permanent call is debilitating. Stay fresh. Find ways to let breezes blow over you. Keep your life minty green.

205. My friend writes poetry and sells gaskets—puts poetry into his work and gaskets into his poetry. His harmonizing rhythm keeps him fresh.

206. Action begets action. It's easier to keep going than get going. When you start, don't get discouraged and quit before you hit stride.

207. Whenever you set a goal, ask yourself: "Is this a goal or a wish?" A goal, you say! Well, then, is it a goal for today or for another time?

208. When you set an authentic goal, this begins the flowering of your resilience.

209. Living up to your potential doesn't get it. You're more textured, deeper, and richer than what society or "time-in-history" say you ought to be.

210. Who and what you are make up what's worth being—not some lie that *says* who you are that you've been believing.

Fear

Is fear our most impeding quality?
I say yes. True,

we're taught rightly from birth
that fear can serve us well.
We know those times and
circumstances. So be it. Yet

what undermines us is fear's adult
falsehood—epidemic among us—
lies licking at our throats, a blade below
whittling away at our health till

the day we die, even hastening
that date. Even sooner, begun
in the garden of the hesitating
attitude, kudzu at the feet
of our life purpose. We've

nurtured it by crafting
our shoulds, oughts and tries.
Good intentions, the sideshow,
purpose the main event.
Yours. What's yours? Oh,

those distractions, the busiest
person on earth absorbed with
all but the one place where
he must put his eye.

Week 31

Your Life's a Poem. What's the Lifeline?

211. Many of us are like fine, old furniture that's been painted over.

212. Be the best, they say! Best at what? Best to whom? Best for how long? Best for sure? How about best for you?

213. Insist on denying your shortcomings, and it will be impossible—down deep—to acknowledge your strengths. Declare.

214. Open 'n' lopin', that's the way! Free and easy with the blinders off. Knowing. Choosing. Your ticket to ride.

215. I like poetry because it's a way of saying what we're not inclined to say—in a few words. What would yours say about you? Try it.

216. Another tack. You can't sail a boat while in harbor. Shove off.

217. Bright, lazy people know how to set priorities. Is that you? No? Fine. Then what? Come to life. Draw the line. Walk it.

Contrarian

The wise woman said to the . . .

bully, weep
speaker, listen
leader, follow
giver, withhold
teacher, learn
clergyman, broaden
poet, capture
CEO, settle
advisor, pace
observer, act
writer, speak
traveler, stay
strong, yield
braggart, confess
pilgrim, invite
seen, see
initiator, wait
taker, give
photographer, blink

contrarian, die

and so she did
and *lived*.

Week 32

See What Others Don't See

218. Patience is passive? Try withdrawing from work you know like the back of your hand to wait and prepare for opportunities that scare you.

219. Last week I spoke of poetry. Here's another take: Writing the poem is the student teaching the teacher.

220. "Like a fanatic, I lay my life on the altar of rabid justification," says he ever so poetically. Ah, he sees his rampant willfulness!

221. Remember the man in the night (week 19)? Therapists to whom he's drawn have a saying: "To know the dream, you have to know the dreamer."

222. "Here I am, 58 years old, and I don't know what I'm going to do when I grow up." Peter Drucker, writing in, say, about 1968. Died at 94. So, live!

223. Savvy people sense the movement of the still stream.

224. Crack lightning, whipping rain all day, creaked the house full with lament. Before the fire, feet planted, our books in our laps. Taken.

189

Corner

Sitting in a corner
as yesteryear's punished
little student, supposedly
a poor cramped example?

Or standing at the intersection
full of options, waiting
for someone or a bus,
maybe merely lingering?

What if you defied the rules,
bringing deep-forced perceptions
from the schoolroom's wedge, stood up,
turned around, pushed the chair aside?

Seeing amply more
than who saw you?
What's declared inside you?
Where are you wanted?

Week 33

Intuition Is the Way

225. Know who give what you value and value what you give. They are pearls of great price.

226. Be heard, not for the sake of democracy, but for your inner truth that is yours alone—and now can become ours.

227. Intuition is the source of all true knowing and understanding. Please, listen to yourself!

228. Don't apologize. Don't explain. Don't defend yourself. All are a waste of effort and a distraction from your inner truth.

229. If you have average intelligence and call upon your intuition, you'll be of more use to society than brilliant people who ignore theirs.

230. How is it that when we add up several small decisions of ours, they somehow *anticipated* what was ahead?

231. My own experience is that my rational voice lies to me, and my inner or intuitive voice never does.

Stealth

The cat, bowed so sweetly
over the saucer of milk,
resting lightly on those little
feet that Sandburg made known,
planted in our heads forever.
The fog of boredom
or listlessness
or loss of place
or an inert mind
may also come in on little cat feet,
and how gracious that is,
for a noisy entrance would
force us to run
from knowing ourselves
in ways that only silence
and aloneness can reveal.

Week 34

When You're Taking It All Too Seriously

232. Awake maybe 10 minutes, barely moving, luxuriating. Amazing! After a whole night, it still feels so good to be just here.

233. Say "WHOA!" Things seem out of balance. You're jumpy, irritable, one-track mind. Some symptom pops up. Your posture declines.

234. Real humor is seeing yourself as the fall guy in the story or joke that makes you laugh.

235. I can't say enough good about meditation. Don't knock it till you've tried it. It can raise your peace quotient.

236. Senses alive! Do you hear the geese flying over, honking bliss? Michelangelo shouted "Breathe, damn you!" when completing *Moses*.

237. Wonder without ambition, something like "I wonder what the purpose is of a covered bridge."

238. Be a child. Count the cars in the next freight train that goes by—the one that stalls your travel to an important meeting.

Dispersed

I need to spread out
like the bands of an
old clock wound tight.
I need to tick tock
out—walk away,
down the stairs,
tell the time without care,
walk the fields
of tall grass without paths,
grab the silty sand
with my hand
under the warm water
at the shore
and shudder with joy
its slipping through my fingers,
feeling my toes
sinking in beneath me.
I need to hold
an ice-cream cone,
sit in an Adirondack chair,
lean back, feel its ribs
and watch
an old lady walk by
leaning on her cane.
Smile at her, speak,
and she to me.
The clock ticks,
no longer mine.

Week 35

Lean into Clarity

239. Turn your pet ideas upside down. Call on a couple of creative friends. One may even jerk you up hard, help you retain the best of you.

240. Get clear! You, as many others, may think charisma is *it*. Not! Claim your true convictions. Pure stances have their own allure.

241. Laugh as you lean. Then throw your head back. This is about joy. Make this your game. Your sights are clear.

242. Keep it simple, like the man who invented the wing nut—just a simple twist between your thumb and forefinger. Snug.

243. Destiny calls. Remember, that's revelation, and a road. It will take turns and test you. You will be better off.

244. Redefine patience as trusting the Divine Mystery.

245. Willfulness is not your friend.

Appearances

I thought I'd light
a candle from the bottom.
Never mind there
was no oxygen, it worked!

When it burned to the top
there was this wide open
cylinder below.
I grabbed the fire hose
from Engine Company #9,
rammed it down the empty shaft
and on this inferno of an
August afternoon, sprayed it on
all the Dalmatians within the
12 rings of the kingdom,
and all was as glorious as if
we were standing knee-deep in
Rome's Trevi Fountain.

The tail wagging sent out cool breezes.
The yipping enlivened the populace.
Torpor was conquered.
Charisma won again.
The King was hanged.

Week 36

Read Books That Get Inside You

246. There's more to read than you can read. Don't read a book just because someone tells you to. Read only what thrills you to know.

247. Fall in love with the author. Be grateful she is teaching you what you want to master.

248. Share your learning with others who are like-minded. They will learn from you and challenge your thoughts so that you'll have to dig deeper.

249. Read fiction as well as nonfiction. Novelists and poets stun us with their truth-telling and insightful array of literary skills.

250. Great stories (fictitious and real) and their lessons will stay with you for life.

251. Less is more. A few good books are better than a batch of bad ones. Bad for *you,* that is!

252. If you're a slow reader, as I am, and it took you a bit longer to learn something significant that's now a part of your life, does that matter?

Book

There's a book lying on their end table,
under the lamp, next to the sofa.
I can't see its cover; it just catches my eye
as I'm leaving, saying good-bye to my host.

It's not a thick book; 250 pages, I'd say,
or maybe a little more. It's not new, either.
Perhaps it stood on a shelf for some years,
saving its little corner in this reader's mind.
There's a postcard, likely sent by a friend,
that keeps the reader's place about a third
of the way through.

I smile to myself with a darting thought
as I step through the door:

"In this our Video Day,
what is more interactive,
significantly interactive,
than holing up
with a book you love
and being loved
by the book you hold?"

It's been said that civilization dates
from the time words appeared on "paper,"
and became portable, reusable—in a way,
broadcast.

Yes. Nice. Necessary.
But O, still, the blessed aloneness of it all,
when I'm arrested by a line, say, from Rainer Maria Rilke,
a character who haunts from Flannery O'Connor,
a mind-bending concept on Job from Stephen Mitchell,
fiction or nonfiction ticklers from Annie Dillard.

Anything—let it be anything
that makes me wonder—for what?

Week 37

Take Stock When You're Cut Off

253. What is it that you always come in second or third? When the recruiter says it's between you and another guy, it's the other guy.

254. When people give you soft answers to this question, or others like it, insist on hard ones. If you show you're serious about this, they'll shoot straight.

255. Ask the same questions of your spouse, closest friend, and blunt sister. They know you well.

256. Quitting makes it harder to start next time. If you quit, it's because you want to. If you want to, it's because you're discouraged.

257. Face the feedback. Finalists are victors. They devote themselves to competence. *Finalist* has the same root as *fine*. Be fine!

258. Sometimes winners lose by winning. Sometimes losers win by losing. It can be confusing, but time often reveals the reasons why.

259. There's a bigger picture, too. Sometimes it's just another person's turn, or simply not yours. I call it Destiny. Feel fortunate.

Sculpture

There is mercy
in the cutoff,
much that we
can never know.
How was it
when I got sick
and couldn't play
the vital games?
How did I fare
when told I
talked too much
and wouldn't present
for our firm?
What did I ask
myself
when she was gone?

Week 38

When Things Get in the Way

260. Recount a time or two when an interruption saved you from an embarrassment at least or, at worst, going over the cliff.

261. Better to be discouraged in the middle than in the beginning. You might create a turning point. There's no turning point at the beginning.

262. Unresponsive to Sara's work this week? Nothing wrong with her work? You were just distracted? Your disengagement got in the way.

263. Many executives aren't into lifelong learning. They think they are but aren't. Serve your career best by putting yourself to some test.

264. There's a strategic side to patience, an affirmation to it that means you can be in charge of your life and work. Assert your patience.

265. You can't always make things happen as you want. Only charlatans profess this and fools believe it. You can never be an always performer.

266. Is your compass pointed in the wrong direction? Has the latest in a string of interruptions shown you so?

Interruption

You'd never guess I, Interruption,
have anything to do with maturity.
I just don't look the part
and that suits me fine.
I'm all about surprise. O,

don't get me wrong, I have
    nothing to do with anybody's
        resolve or refusal to grow; I'm just
            one of the underrated influences
                sent by God, or as some

more fashionable
than I would say, fate.
But I'm the one who does
the job, knows who sent me,
and I'm no accident.

My nickname is Needle, and
    my point makes the tip
        of Sir Galahad's lance
            seem as blunt as a boxer's glove.
                The space I pierce sometimes

would defy detection
by an electron microscope,
yet I'm often present to
prick one's balloon the size
of a dirigible. You know from

experience I have a sense
   of humor and can be as ironic
      as a rainbow . . . my message
         as clear as a firehouse bell:
            Stop. See what you're missing.

Week 39

Make Memories Work for You

267. You always have the power to remember.

268. Take the time to remember. You have to relax to do this. Believe me, you have the time.

269. Remembering is not living in the past. It's learning from the past, what may have been forgotten, and refreshing it for the present.

270. There are those who dwell in the "good old days" but you know from my spirit that's not what we're about here!

271. Here's a question: Think back on a rich time in your youth. What did it have that's missing in your life now? Bring it back in new form.

272. Even bad memories won't do you in. Don't be afraid to go there. Stare it down, find out that its sting is gone. What's the learning?

273. Some event in your past flashes pure delight. That flash is you. Act on it and you'll capture what's unique and worthwhile in you.

Facings

Memories the last four days:

1.

A smile, what is this one
among all kinds?
She's lifted her eyes, looking
at something through the transom.
I see first her lower teeth, then up—
a pleasing smile, one that quickens
my blood and pulls me forward
out of my chair.
I stand behind her
with my arms around her waist,
pull her close to me.

2.

Swimming playfully in the Atlantic,
off the Georgia coast, underwater,
eyes open, 40 feet or so from shore,
I'm startled to see a stingray glide by
at arms length, whipping its tail.

Terrified, can you imagine?
The thought of a bee sting
hurls me into a downward whirl
of projected pain I've never felt!
I swim to shore frantically
and stand looking back,
betrayed by my knees.

3.

Ho, you simple garter snake black
with pale yellow and coral stripes atop,
and greenish-white underbelly
that my friends and I discovered.
Gasped and stepped back, we did,
when we lifted a flat rock out of the mud.
You wriggled so when I grasped you
right behind your head—
your tongue lashing out
with the speed
of a woodpecker's hammer,
our first time, fright-jammed revelation.
Pitching you forward
like a rejected small fish,
we watched you disappear
into the tall grass as water
sinks into sand.

Sure you weren't poisonous,
in later days we went looking
for your brothers—a time-limited dive,
a short season in the tenth year
of a boy's adventure. But here,
now, comes meandering
that fat time,
your return, in memory,
received gratefully,
with vivid fears, awe
of your slim gracefulness.

4.

A seagull in Del Mar
circles over the water,
swoops and glides
inward above land, turns,
descends smoothly to the beach,
flaps to a quick, smooth landing
and for a few proud moments
stands at attention.
She knows
I've been
with
her?

Whatever happens. Whatever
what is is is what
I want. Only that. But that.

—*Galway Kinnell*

The tagline for resourcefulness is *find a way.* For me, resourcefulness and creativity are two sides of the same coin. Both require imagination and receptivity. The people who are receptive to ideas from others are just as creative as the givers. In the last analysis, the receiver has to make a judgment of the likelihood of success in employing the suggested idea. How does it truly fit with the challenge framed up by her? How skillfully has she stated the issue to be faced and the guidelines laid out in an inspiring way? How adaptable and perceptive is she when subjected to a proposed solution far afield from anything she had in mind? How *creative* is she as she noodles it over for a few days and finds a way to get past the resistance likely to come from her peers? Be creative. Make it resourceful.

Week 40

Time to Participate in the Everyday

274. So much I would learn reaches my eyes and ears, but not my heart. What then?

275. I heard a sound this week that had gone out of my life: the slamming of a screen door.

276. Change is changing to whom we are. *That* change threads its way into the observations of others.

277. Has it sunk in that the room grew silent when I said *no*?

278. I just wonder what's behind our hanging-bite love of the open road.

279. If it's adequate, really adequate, it's adequate.

280. I see no entangled prey, so I'm thinking that today the spider's job is maintenance.

Moments

Just after I
get into bed
I hear a fat drop
smack the bottom
of the downspout
outside our bedroom,
echoing in the
small courtyard.
It's a welcome sound
even though it may
foreshadow
an overcast and
hindering tomorrow.
I lie there and
listen as the pace
quickens like soldiers
stepping up their cadence;
then all is quiet
as the flow is full.
I go to the open window
to see the street
glistening and watch
a car go by,
feeling on my forearms
the hiss of its spinning tires,
then settle back to bed,
sifting into the sweet rhythm.

Week 41

This Growth Thing Is Up to You

281. Development is making no excuses, placing no blame.

282. Life is sometimes like holding a bushel basket the rain runs through. It won't hold the water, but it's cleaner from the action.

283. Failing is seeing how you fell short and where your growth is from here.

284. Accomplishing is temporary. A good turn here is an opportunity to evaluate so-called success.

285. Loving is the only way to find out what in life you're being asked to do.

286. Striving is one of the best ways I know how to miss the point.

287. Modeling is showing how you do it well while keeping your mouth shut.

Bal-Hoola

I've been to Bal-Hoola
      don't ask me to say
      would you want to go there?
      then be on your way

I've been to Bal-Hoola
      don't ask me to say
      what does a lad learn there?
      will make a man gray

I've been to Bal-Hoola
      how long is the road?
      I've warned you before
      your question's a goad

I've been to Bal-Hoola
      there's mercy there
      does that surprise you
      O, you with such flair?

I've been to Bal-Hoola
> their questions are strong
> how do we gain wisdom?
> by seeing we're wrong

I've been to Bal-Hoola
> and I've said my piece
> you can't go to Bal-Hoola
> without signing the lease

I've returned to Bal-Hoola
> that says it all
> there's no true travel
> short of heeding the call

Week 42

How Will You Define Your Leadership?

288. Because life across its full spectrum requires endless variability and flexibility, change is our constant.

289. Little things, particularly when they run together, send out the big messages.

290. Leadership, like beauty, is in the eye of the beholder. It always requires an adjective. Strong leader. Weak leader.

291. Live today, today, but not only for today.

292. Would you and your associates like to debate something over coffee? Try this: "Human nature never changes."

293. Play with ideas, yes, but before you get to the real playground—the joy-space—comes blood, sweat, and tears.

294. Word game—ten to live by, ending in *ty*: veracity, tenacity, alacrity, variety, levity, brevity, humility, felicity, sensitivity, ability.

Magic

There's a rush
that comes
in the presence
of a true talent—
a creativity that
smacks me down flat
as a squirrel in a hard storm.
I say to such
an executive,
let me share something,
then I do,
then she says,
say more,
then I do,
then she sees
the critical edge
in her power
and acts on herself
to move the needle,
and out comes the rabbit.
It's that simple.

Week 43

Juice Up the Ordinary

295. Architect Louis Sullivan wrote "Form ever follows function." Grasp true function, not good intentions, and you'll juice up a lot of dry dirt.

296. I seek signs and feelings for what wins my heart for our abode, each day. How do we bend—our house and us—to meet our functions?

297. The day begins with a small, slow upward step. In my mind's eye, a calla lilly on the rise—as if in time-lapse photography, to set my pace.

298. See him see her now, taking a nap, tiny triangle of her face covered by the crumpled sheet, eyes, nose, lips, serene, peeking pretty.

299. Here's the thing about a poem: It doesn't always behave. In fact, it can grow wild in its development—just like you.

300. The cargo box carries contents; accepts handling, mobility, recycling; gives itself thanklessly to anticipated delight on arrival.

301. The grandfather clock: Many choice nights, sleeping alone, I have waited—not restlessly— for its sure clang at the foot of the stairs.

Cocktail

It's my favorite.
I named it "The Sod Glacier."

2 oz of Old Bushmills plain label Irish Whiskey,
poured over hard fresh rocks in a short glass
that fits my hand perfectly.

Why do I like it so?
This beverage is caringly crafted
by sod-busting leprechauns
in the world's oldest distillery
and offers see-through simplicity.

It presents itself with earth-tone warmth,
signifying grounding.
Yet it is paired adeptly with the copious ice
that fills the resplendent glass
and delivers sincerity
side-by-side
with cold, hard, dispassionate clarity.

It is most enjoyed when seated well
at day's end,
reflecting on the joys of one's labors
or applying finishing touches
to the formulation of a great idea.

Week 44

Chart a Brief Early Bio

302. "Just realize where you come from: this is the essence of wisdom." —*Tao Te Ching*

303. Get down on paper those formative and most memorable events of your first 10–15 years of your life.

304. Don't labor over this. Spread the task out over a reflective week or two. Let come what may. Just bullet the high and low points.

305. Mull them over, for better or worse. Have you been remaking history through your memory? Assigning blame? Making excuses? Check it out.

306. Whom do you love and "owe" your gratefulness? Your expanded thoughts and feelings are what count. Use that yellow pad.

307. Who/what scared you? Your expanded thoughts and feelings, please. Delight or fright . . . from here on, which will win your might?

308. When did you soar? What tells you what your special gifts are? How will you go about expressing them now? They haven't gone away.

Boy

A man may grow up
forgetting he was a boy,
or thinking he forgot.
Certainly there was
much to remember,
but also the impulse
to put behind.
Three generations
and a kid brother in two
houses side by side with a
handful of boarders to boot.
Now he's moved east
with his master's degree
and scarcely a thought
of skinned knees,
climbing the cherry tree
and the hurt amid tears
when his best friend
moved away, a father
who ran alongside the
learning biker, then let go,

the mother and grandmother
who could cook up a dream
and place it on the table,
a grandfather who taught him
how to whittle and held him close,
the kid brother who sassed him right.
The revisits that recur
at times unexpected
will warm the walls
of his Park Avenue office
and give him a spine
for the missing rainbows.

Week 45

What Am I Doing Here?

309. Energy is a result of naming what you care about. If you can't name it, you can't act on it.

310. Sometimes we're afraid to name what we care about because we'll be asked to act on it and fear failing at it.

311. There are cycles—times for flying high and laying low. In times of confusion, just stay put for a while. Lean back with no apologies.

312. Grow young now. Turn an emotional somersault or two. Take yourself back to the park when you were ten. What's in you wanting to come out?

313. Ask yourself what, exactly, your organization wants done. Ask if you're a person who can help deliver it. Yes?

314. Then ask if this is the time to do it or would its timing be better later. Let's say now!

315. Then ask: "In tandem with what people should I take this on?" and go round them up.

Staying

Come, to hear.
Hear what?
Hear what's inside you.
Strange you would
say that.
It puts me in a cloud cover:
silence, seeing nothing either.
You know me better
than anyone,
lost, now,
the champion miler.
Your being here
shuts me down,
yet don't go away.
I have to start all over,
knowing nothing.
Let me just lean backward
against this rock.
I look across the sand.
the cloud lifted,
to the sea and feel its
soft surf coming and going.
This inlet bluff that supports
me says nothing.

Week 46

Claim Your Underpinning

316. What do you count on? When everything falls apart, where do you turn? Serious illness. Lost job. Gone broke. A loved one dies.

317. What could it mean to have a river beneath you? In a way, it could be just the same as earth, another presence of nature holding you up.

318. The notion of being held up—supported—grates on us some because we don't like to think of ourselves as being so dependent—weak, even.

319. The close call is a reminder, perhaps just temporarily, of our vulnerability, when we escape some tragedy by a thin margin.

320. That river, ground, or community that bears you up is yours to claim and love daily because life is never without its fragility.

321. For most on the globe, that underpinning is a faith or spirituality of some stripe whether or not we're formal practitioners.

322. Claim that underpinning however you can.

River

There came a top line from a shuttered old hymn
on a low wind from nowhere this morning,
and drizzled cool on the top of my head,
that brought sharp sweet chill to my bearing:

When peace like a river attendeth my way . . .

Forget religion and
lie down softly on the word.
If I were a teacher
I would ask for silence
and have the students
say the line
over to themselves
as a secular chant.

Oh, there's Whitehead again,
peering over my shoulder:
"Seek simplicity and distrust it."
Who can argue with him?
Yet this morning, at least,
and I must admit—
amid no great strife,
there was a river.

Week 47

Learning Is Your Dance of Life

323. Some of our best learning is unlearning—when we learn what we thought was true, isn't.

324. Some of our best knowing is not knowing—when we have "beginners mind."

325. "I am still learning." —*Michelangelo* at age 87

326. Learners are the best teachers.

327. Often our best answer to life is a question.

328. Dialogue is learning.

329. Silence is learning

Dancers

I have a set of bookends fierce in their reach.

I see and feel them as
Icons—ical ones—Spiritual.

Their texture is rough to
the hand—cold, heavy
black steel castings. Identical.
Naked, looking-to-be Giacometti men
with slim muscular bodies.

Bookends keep books in—keep them from sliding;
falling over, making a mess.
That's their work, applying pressure.

These do more than that,
though, you'll see.
They are seated firmly,
solemn eyes outward,
buttocks against the books,
backs leaning straight,
legs crossed at the ankle,
left over right.

Opposites, you know the look;
in one you see his sole,
the other his locked ankle.
Maximum force would be
both feet planted on the shelf,
bracing, no give—back and
upper arms tense.

Yet they're not relaxing—crossed legs
almost always betray angst—and there's
a shading of movement here, man and book
intermingled, both tension and a drawing upon
mutual support—for now, most supplied
by the men.

Listen, though, for these men are
journeymen—as St. Paul was a tent-maker
for hire—producers, adequacy known and
paid for when I brought them home from the store.

But more—much more lies in wait
for them—as it was with St. Paul,
by leaning on the books as he
leaned on the knee of Gamaliel—
his teacher . . .

Through their backs—that
precious contact—their leaning
strength of inquiry, and belief,
from just this bent, they draw out
into their pores wisdom, ease, patience,

and rise when I sleep,
to live, and dance the teaching,
and the Word and Art
become one, giving
me yet another chance.

Week 48

Your Spiritual Journey:
Current Propositions

330. For You? Perhaps? Today's spiritual quest rises from a deep well, brick-lined and more sturdy than the "New Age" base of recent years.

331. "Spirituality" is not retreat from established religion, as much as engaged dialogue and distinction between what we thought and what we now think.

332. Life's mysteries are acknowledged, not dismissed. Energized explorers share differences and commonalities in their faith (or lack of it).

333. Faith questions and life's mysteries are as likely of being examined by the university's physics department as its school of religion.

334. This firm quest is budding among the pilgrims: Ethics, integrity, authenticity, and soul are not the sole province of organized religion.

335. So now we have among us an enlivening give-and-take. No two people worship the same God—even when we're talking about the same God.

336. Hordes dropped out from tradition. After this muscular inquiry, many returned to a new home, citizens in the larger, timeless world.

Transit

I heard it with my own ears from Walter Brueggemann, a friend
and Old Testament scholar: a fellow St. Louis Cardinal fan.

God is in recovery from violence.

I was as startled as a philanderer caught naked. I didn't ask
what he meant; there wasn't time, and then, it's more perverse
to do my own plumbing on his broken-pipe gusher. How many
wandering would-be pilgrims have lived, and nations of
wayfarers will be born to a new gaggling line? O, my, earth time
and Kingdom time—such a difference beyond our grasp: Do I
have this right —a thousand years is an instant in God's eye? What
the hell does that mean, except

yes, oh yes, there's time for recovery.

Ever wonder why He/She/It waited 15 billion years to put us in charge
of this little, round ball? Given our mess it seems the only secret on
violence may lie in the fact that our omni-God *needs us* for recovery!
Sounds absurd, I know, but answer me: What arms will wrap like vines
around God's tree? Eyes narrow at a purple dawn? Faces shine at a child's
birth? Tears flow as from a stabbed heart at a soldier's death? Whose
trust expressed in tomorrow?—

if not ours?

Hard to believe God's counting on us, but if this preposterous leak of recognition has any merit, based on the patience God has shown, might it
someday be a gusher of its own? Is it seeping as an underground stream below our bodies and bears us skimming across all interior surfaces each century, an inch closer to the truth? Are a thousand years really an instant?
If so, then that makes Eternity the time of times, and what, do tell, does that mean? Could it mean we're already there, working at recovery,

practicing the eternal propositions? Perhaps. See below my lights—some of them sprinkled earlier in the weekly seven tweets . . .

Ultimately, seeking power fails.

Let all illusions go.

Yielding is the way of wisdom.

The right thing is the appropriate thing.

Everyone needs to go through dark nights of the soul.

Impatient, you can ruin what almost arrived.

Each is one with the universe.

If we don't forgive our enemies, we become *them*.

The future causes the present.

There are times to trust people who aren't trustworthy.

Learn from the wise and step out on your own.

Life lived too intensely is life lived poorly.

"Let it happen" wears better than "Make it happen."

Take your stand, then be quiet.

A flipped penny can shape alternatives as much as any larger coin.

If you want to know what people (including yourself) are committed to, don't listen to their words. See where their feet take them.

Geography is destiny.

If God, the All, has always existed and always will, then we are participating in eternity right now.

The shortest distance between two points is a straight line, but attentive meandering often brings superior results.

Collaboration without consensus is the soul of organizational truth.

It's up and down on the merry-go-round.

Small decisions confirm a larger agenda.

Nothing has to be possible. Anything can be possible.

Truly great ideas don't come of age without debate.

Good intentions are a substitute for performance.

Permanence is proof of adaptability, so far.

One of life's most serviceable questions is "Says who?"

A value is what we live by, not merely profess, whether it's positive or negative.

In due time, the wolf and the lamb shall feed together.

Week 49

Get Off to a Good Start

337. The time has come in our journey: Start your engines!

338. Do people draw strength from you? Are they fed from your nature or drained by it? Be a nurturer, not an impairer.

339. Have you learned how to be a team leader? Team member? These skills must be learned. Not? Now is soon enough.

340. Running meetings well is essential for team leadership. Ask candid associates what they think of the meetings you run.

341. You're layers beneath your CEO? Your job: Contribute to the generation of ideas. Do it and your work soon will be felt upwards.

342. CEOs are on the lookout for team-builders. They know 'em when they see 'em. Be one and you'll be seen.

343. Think of team in everything you do. Your individual effort is critical as ever, but merely your expression of the team *apart*.

Depth

Slow down, he says.
Find your place slowly.
Speed must be for spurts,
I think, then,
because his words,
not just the content,
sound husky, dry,
learned, like corn
in the wind.
I see him see
what he sees,
hear what he hears,
walk what he walks.
I think, then, yes,
speed must be spurts—
a call for the swift,
deft swing of the sword,
timely, not over-employed.
Walk it, don't talk it.
People will know
you're coming.

Week 50

Time to Get Rid of the Options

344. Wolf wanted sweeter grapes high on the vine. To have them, he'd have to unclench the grapes in his teeth and leap. He wouldn't do it.

345. The school nurse spilled coins across the floor. She started to pick up one, then went to another and another without picking up any.

346. A CEO had a golden egg, but the goose was getting old. No new products replaced the egg; the goose died and the company with her.

347. We clutch options that block growth and elect options that keep us from pure pursuit of our central purpose.

348. Too many options hedge the bet and don't place the bet.

349. "Stay loose," he says. No! Get tight on this and go for it.

350. "Anyone who's not fired with enthusiasm will be fired with enthusiasm." —*Vince Lombardi*

Slide

Heel and toe, heel and toe,
slide, slide, slide.
I'm thinking of things
that slide, or if you prefer—
glide.
The movement is smooth
but also rigidly controlled:
Tongue-in-groove carpentry.
A river's normal flow
within its banks.
Airplanes in their lanes—
their glide-paths coming in.
Heavy machines in a plant,
on rails, moving easily,
with precision
to where needed.
Submarine torpedoes
slotted into place
for firing.

Making love.
William Blake wrote,
and I agree,
"Improvement makes
straight roads; but the
crooked roads without
improvement are
roads of genius."
But today, for awhile
at least, I'm sunk deep
in the ways I want
to be controlled
to superior purpose.

Week 51

Reinvent Yourself and Don't Look Back

351. "If you aren't afraid of dying, there is nothing you can't achieve." *Tao Te Ching.* Dying to preconceptions, that is.

352. The force of a resistant will is paltry in the face of a true calling.

353. Self-image is often a lie. Often, we aren't who we tell ourselves we are.

354. Perversely, what scares us the most are those tasks that prove exhilarating when we lower our heads and gut them through.

355. Tunefully now: "Oh where oh where has my little self gone, oh where oh where can it be?"

356. Yes, it's clear to me this instant, reinventing myself is a task of reclamation, not revision.

357. "Change occurs when we become who we are, not when we try to become who we're not." —*Arnold Beisser, M.D.*

Expectations

What you thought was, wasn't.
What you think is, isn't.
It's like putting out
a new idea, but the last
words won't come
and your listener
completes it for you.
Yes, Yes, you exclaim.
Until you arrive you can't know
the "that's it," and perhaps
not then either since the arrival,
chidingly so, is a new beginning.
Change a person's expectations,
we say, and you can change *them*.
Well, yes again, just so . . .
Expectations have kept me
from seeing what's there.
What I thought was, wasn't
and I'm new eyes ready.

Week 52

Your Course Is Clear

358. "I am like all other men. I am like some other men. I am like no other man." Listen to Aeschylus. On and off the job, express *no-other-person* qualities.

359. Separate your unique strengths from your "me-too" strengths and act on *them*.

360. Accept your gifts? "Hey, you're good at that," she says. "Oh, come on," you say." "No, I mean it." "Really?" you say.

361. To be good at something puts you on the spot. It means you can't malinger. People expect good things from you.

362. If you've shown you're good with some gift, and the reactions of others won't let you hide from that, bathe in it, claim it. It's you.

363. Your mission: biting statement of purpose, uniqueness, and method. 75 words max. First sentence brief, inspiring, and memorable.

364. Go for it. "The man of courage flees forward," said Jacques Maritain—a life-yielding spurt from the inert . . .

One

Let me count the ways . . .

No!

Look
Listen
Think
Feel
Now
Me

There is only one way.

365. See the four emotions—mad, glad, sad, and afraid. Where will you point your life? Be *there*. Be a reason for gladness.

Ease

The great move
is the appropriate.
It makes life
without effort,
churning but a memory.
If one can forget about gain
and somehow be appropriate,
gain becomes the ready companion.
Joy leaps to the center,
spontaneity the flash,
receptivity the guideline.
What is the picture today,
how am I in it
or out of it?
When do I paint,
when am I painted?
She's so good, she
doesn't know it!
What does that mean?
you ask.
The popular answer?
Flow.
Not so popular?
The right fit —
Destiny's cure with
no strings attached.

Acknowledgments

Several people lent their gifts to make this book what it is. Michael Stern, Big B Consulting, was an ideal guide who offered incisive evaluations of our publishing alternatives and skillfully managed the book's editing, layout, and jacket design. My wife, Cher, has the enlivened eye and provided the arresting photographs for each chapter and the book jacket, and in so doing, advanced the message.

Chapter 48, *Your Spiritual Journey*, the book's longest chapter, came together from several sources. Old Testament scholar and friend Walter Brueggemann bowled me over in a lecture with his statement "God is in recovery from violence," and I was off on the topic. One night a bit later, Fourth Presbyterian Church of Chicago conducted what they call "The Michigan Avenue Forum," and 1,200 people packed the place to hear Eboo Patel interview Krista Tippett onstage. Krista is host of National Public Radio's popular *On Being*, and Eboo is president of *Interfaith Youth Core* and an American Muslim. The pair was perfectly matched by Eboo's serving up penetrating questions and Krista's returning clear, persuasive responses. Their revealing conversation on the spiritual shifts of our day helped shape my wording of the tweets that introduce this chapter.

Cher's cover photograph of the sculpture *Stallone* is one she took as we strolled along the shore of Lake Lugano in Switzerland. I was stunned by the power of the work and saw that it captured what I mean by *WHOA!* in the book's title. Cher went tracking to see who was the creator of this magnificent piece and learned it was Nag Arnoldi, the renowned and beloved Swiss artist. I got in touch with him, and he graciously, immediately, gave permission to use the photograph for the jacket.

I am deeply grateful as well to my accomplished colleague, Sona Chawla, President of E-Commerce for Walgreens. Anyone familiar with the rapid, imaginative growth of the Big Red W's online services knows fully that the complexity she addresses in her Foreward is what she faces daily on behalf of this $72 billion sales pharmacy/retail colossus. That a book like this might offer grounding amid such a challenging climate is music to my ears.

Appendix A

As mentioned in the Introduction, an empty yellow pad is a great companion on your journey to reclaiming your authenticity. It's a great place to store your notes and doodle new ideas that come to you as you read *WHOA!*

This is a 52-week program. Don't rush it. These sample Worksheets were created to help you get started jotting things down and guide you into a rhythm. You'll develop your own style of note taking.

I suggest you commit to spending one hour each week to reading the tweets, reviewing the photography and interpreting the poetry. Maybe it's Tuesday's during your lunch hour. Maybe it's early Sunday morning for an hour. Maybe it's with a cup of tea before you leave the office on a set day each week. Maybe it's with a glass of wine at the end of the day. Your call. This book is to help you on the path to making your life more meaningful to the people you care about most. That's the "They."

Once you've done these exercises, perhaps this is something your organization should do collectively as a project.

What discussion groups could come out of this?

Should you have a Weekly Luncheon Discussion Group for 52 weeks and see how to cross pollinate ideas and help one another be better spouses, parents, colleagues, friends?

I'd be flattered to speak to your management team. Thanks for joining me on the journey.

Allan Cox
email: allan@allancox.com

WORKSHEET

for

WHOA! Are They Glad You're in Their Lives?
by Allan Cox

1

Week Number _____ Date _____

2

Write the first thing that comes to your mind.
You can always change it later.

*Given how I see myself today,
my purpose in life is*

_____

_____

3

Key people in my life:

*(Make it long; do not limit the list to only the
lines below.)*
Include spouse, kids, peers,
colleagues/associates, siblings, parents, and
others.

_____	_____
_____	_____
_____	_____
_____	_____
_____	_____

READ THE TWEETS

What does the chapter title say to you right off?
(You are free to change your mind later on.)

_____

Read each tweet. Take time to mentally digest it.

No._____   Tweet_____

What does it say to you?

_____

What do they (this week's tweets) make you thing about the way you work?

_____

How can you improve the way you work?

_____

Whom have you drawn into your circle?

_____

Whom have you left out of your circle you need to include?

_____

Who shares your enthusiasm?

_____

Of the seven tweets, which strikes you as the most critical to your life?

No._____   Tweet_____

5

LOOK AT THE PHOTOGRAPH

What does the photo make you think of?

_____

6

READ THE POEM

Where does the poem take you?

_____

7

NOW, LOOK BACK AT THE PHOTO CHOSEN TO ACCOMPANY THE POEM

Why do you think this photo was chosen to accompany the poem?

_____

What do you see?

_____

What does it remind you of?

_____

Does it elicit a particular feeling? If so, what is it?

_____

About Allan Cox

Allan Cox is president and founder of Allan Cox & Associates Inc. He is a CEO advisor and poet-blogger. Cox has authored eight previous books, including the bestsellers *Confessions of a Corporate Headhunter* (the first book ever written about the executive search profession), *Inside Corporate America*, *The Making of the Achiever*, and *The CEO in You*.

He has advised CEOs and top management teams of many corporations and not-for-profit organizations, including USG, Walgreens, Consolidated Communications, Columbus McKinnon, Esmark, Kraft, Pillsbury, Quidel, the Minnesota Vikings, Child Welfare League of America, and *The Christian Century* magazine. He served for five years as Chairman of the Board of Chicago's Center for Ethics and Corporate Policy.

Find Allan at AllanCox.com, Twitter, Facebook, LinkedIn, Scriibd and Red Room.

Photographic Credits

All photographs in this publication, unless otherwise stated, are by Cher Cox.

The photograph of Sona Chawla is by Erik Unger, *Crain's Chicago Business.*

Look for Allan's new book *The CEO in You*

"Allan Cox helps nurture people and corporations the way perceptive executives treat a great brand."

—Wally Olins
Co-founder & Chairman of London-Based Saffron Brand Consultants; author of *On Brand*

"*The CEO in You* takes you beyond theory to commonsense wisdom. Cox's insights are exactly what is needed for the development and release of today's global executive."

—Jan Bubenik
Managing Director, Bubenik Partners, Prague, Czech Republic

Other books by Allan Cox

Redefining Corporate Soul (with Julie Liesse)

Straight Talk for Monday Morning

The Achiever's Profile

The Making of the Achiever

Inside Corporate America

Work, Love and Friendship

Confessions of a Corporate Headhunter

Made in the USA
Lexington, KY
14 June 2012